The Moon Is Always Whole

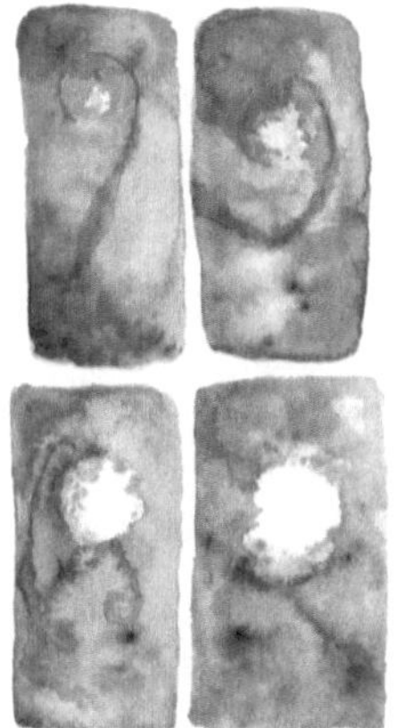

THE DREAMSEEKER POETRY SERIES

Books in the DreamSeeker Poetry Series, intended to make available fine writing by Anabaptist-related poets, are published by Cascadia Publishing House under the DreamSeeker Books imprint and sometimes have been copublished with Herald Press. Cascadia oversees content of these poetry collections in collaboration with the DreamSeeker Poetry Series Editor Jeff Gundy (Jean Janzen volumes 1-4) as well as when called for in consultation with its Editorial Council and the authors themselves.

1 On the Cross
   By Dallas Wiebe, 2005

2 I Saw God Dancing
   By Cheryl Denise, 2005

3 Evening Chore
   By Shari Wagner, 2005

4 Where We Start
   By Debra Gingerich, 2007

5 The Coat Is Thin, 2008
   By Leonard Neufeldt

6 Miracle Temple, 2009
   By Esther Stenson

7 Storage Issues, 2010
   By Suzanne Miller

8 Face to Face, 2010
   By Julie Cadwallader-Staub

9 What's in the Blood, 2012
   By Cheryl Denise

10 The Apple Speaks, 2012
   By Becca J. R. Lachman

Also worth noting are two poetry collections that would likely have been included in the series had it been in existence then:

DreamSeeker Books also continues to release occasional high-caliber collections of poems outside of the DreamSeeker Poetry Series:

1 The Mill Grinds Fine: Collected Poems
   By Helen Wade Alderfer, 2009

2 How Trees Must Feel
   By Chris Longenecker, 2011

The Moon Is Always Whole

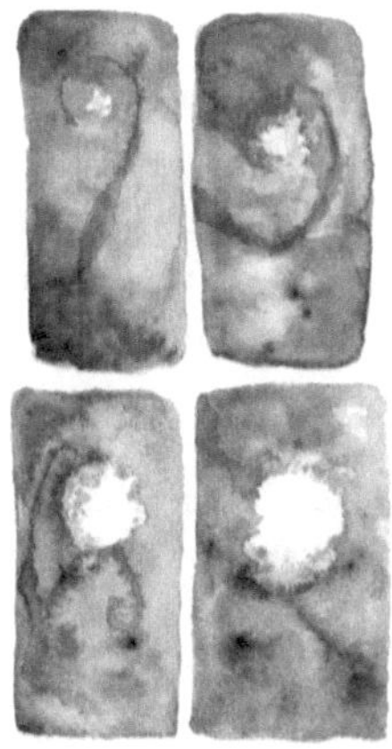

Poems by
Julia Baker Swann

DreamSeeker Poetry Series, Volume 19

DreamSeeker Books
TELFORD, PENNSYLVANIA

an imprint of
Cascadia Publishing House LLC

Cascadia Publishing House orders, information, reprint permissions:
contact@CascadiaPublishingHouse.com
1-215-723-9125
126 Klingerman Road, Telford PA 18969
https://www.CascadiaPublishingHouse.com

The Moon Is Always Whole

DreamSeeker Books is an imprint of Cascadia Publishing House LLC
ISBN 13: 978-1-68027-018-1   ISBN 10: 1-68027-018-4
Book design by Cascadia Publishing House
Cover design by Gwen M. Stamm
Cover design based on watercolor painting "There Through
It All," by Julia Baker Swann

Versions of poems in this collection have appeared in various outlets. For a listing,
see Acknowledgments and Credits section, back of book.

Library of Congress Cataloguing-in-Publication Data

Library of Congress Cataloging-in-Publication Data

Names: Swann, Julia Baker, 1989- author.
Title: The moon is always whole / poems by Julia Baker Swann.
Description: Telford, Pennsylvania : DreamSeeker Books, an imprint of
    Cascadia Publishing House LLC, [2020] | Series: DreamSeeker poetry
    series; volume 19 | Summary: "This collection invites readers into the
    body's rhythms of creation, love, and loss-affirming that even as we see
    only in part, "the moon is always whole" within and beyond chronic
    illness, ancestral trauma, silencing, betrayal"-- Provided by publisher.

Identifiers: LCCN 2020036906 | ISBN 9781680270181 (paperback)
Subjects: LCGFT: Poetry.
Classification: LCC PS3619.W3559 M66 2020 | DDC 811/.6--dc23
LC record available at https://lccn.loc.gov/2020036906

25 24 23 22 21 20   10 9 8 7 6 5 4 3 2 1

In memory of
Seth Bailey Dunn

CONTENTS

2: Waxing

Subsection - Eclipse

(section of untitled poem)

(end section of untitled poem)

"God is a circle, whose center is everywhere and circumference is nowhere."
—Nicholas of Cusa

1

New Moon

I Make in Circles

My finger carves a dewy path on cold glass,
and with sticks a line in the sand,
bent to touch so the end begins.

I lay discarded bits—a dried crab leg, a gull's
flight-feather, a pearl-blue shell, the slick
cord of kelp—into the crease my pressing made.

Yesterday I knelt in clay loam
greened by winter to place petals,
blushed as the peaches to come, in a round.

At five I spun in concerned circles asking my mother
what are other kids doing right now? *What shape am I?*
Told to draw square houses with a triangle roof,

I curved a rainbow over the lines.
I saw the colors of light continue their arc,
spilled through soil and stone,

painting tree roots on the way to completion.
I am in conversation with this light—
gathered in moon and sun,

in these circles I keep making,
to ask the question again and again
a self-portrait made of answers.

Metamorphosis

After the storm, butterflies,
as if birthed from liquid cocoons.

Chrysalis droplets hewn in humid clouds
till thunder rumbles lose a flutter of moths.

Or maybe they rose from below,
fabric bodies rolled in twisted roots

till soil so drunk on warm rain,
orange silk spins to light.

In the streambed I find moth wings,
tissue paper strewn on damp slate.

The body gone, four eyes left,
gilded black circles

look up at me in expectation.
I touch a wing, soft as the fine

hairs on an arm. The artist's hand
painted each gauzy triangle, ochre melds

to cream, brilliant blue, and scarlet of blood,
color stain in dark refuge.

No need to show each step of becoming,
when ready wings unfurl to light.

Conception

Curtis died, bleeding away
after just weeks in utero,
named after a great-grandfather.
They kept a grandfather's
name, David, for a birth.
That fall my mother went into
full-mooned September heat.
In their attic room,
twin beds pushed together,
my parents joined
grief and longing.
On the stretch of San Francisco Bay
early morning fog eased.
Named Julia Lynn
after strong Honduran women,
middle name of my mother
lake, cascade, pool at the bottom,
I entered the waters.

Word Child

After Mai Der Vang's "Mother of People Without Script"

Before missionaries wrote the language down
    Hmong script was nurtured from breath to ear.
I borrow the phrase "*Niam Ntawv*"
    Mother of Paper, Mother of Writing.

Words were milk spilled from my lips,
    now they pour honey-slow,
my soul's quiet birth onto crisp paper.
    Poems are the children I feed.

The Moment I Knew

I was in a hardware store.
Adrift in the faucet aisle,
Daddy and the aproned man—

big hands, big beard,
big laugh, big flat words—
drip and pour of plumbing-ese.

Drowning, my reflection
in polished brass caught me, a voice
without words summoned.

    I saw myself.

Wearing that favorite shirt,
yellow with green flecked leaves
lifted from cotton like braille.

No longer image and yellow,
no longer threads woven,
no longer an eight-year-old's search.

I found Beyond,
what could never be unseen.
Afloat in wonder

I looked back at gestures large and linear
that asked why I was staring into space.
Awash in first loneliness

knowing I could not speak
of *this*,
in that language.

My Home

is built from lavish solitude.

From here I write
all the words it has taken me
so long to come home to.

Mostly silent, save exhales
through heart chimes.

Walls come round me
not to keep in or out,
but to hold the space.

Straw and timber curve.
Each held beam is lily-fair.
Moon rings touch
every corner of the circle.

Windows look out
at the landscape within.

The only furniture
a small desk, paper ready
and lavender in a blue jar.

No need for pattern of clock
or calendar square.

I trust turtle eggs left on sand.
Hatchlings emerge

in the fullness of time

following brightest light
to open sea.

I Come From

For Fresno

I come from zip-lock bags rewashed
hung on the clothesline.
Plastic parachutes filled with smog
and the neighbors' *reggaeton.*
I come from harvesting tomatoes
on Christmas, fruit of seeds
planted in February,
in this place that makes
the "worst cities for..." list every year.
But we grow things—
purslane between the
cracks of Blackstone Ave,
persimmons, and grapes in backyards,
poets and subtle beauty.
I come from sitting on the kitchen floor,
warped plastic linoleum,
the hearth for tears and curiosity.
I come from NPR at 5pm.
All things are considered
in this home grown of intentionality
where you don't leave
the lid off the toothpaste.
I come from details matter
and grace abounds,
all in the same weighty love-doused breath.
I come from air guitar and Bono's voice
"It's a beautiful day...don't let it get away..."
We move quickly when camping gear
is spread on that kitchen floor.

Movements toward our other home
in the Sierras above the crust of baked smog
where we stop under a giant ancestor—
red bark lit from the heavens.

Happiness

as a word is not full enough
  for what I seek.

The dusky desire of ancient stars
  a canticle in me.

This melody is not the prattle
  of a mockingbird's copy-song.

I am the soar
  of a lark's chord.

Dissonant exile
  hums in tension

with consonant belonging.
  Harmony serenades

on the other side of night—
pleasures wail in my throat.

Faithful Moon

it will be established forever like the moon,
the faithful witness in the sky.
—Psalm 89:37

Curled wisp of blonde on Honduran sky,
luna-moona I called her

child-moon out by day.
Milky smudge in a blue bowl,

Stillpoint in this turning,
steady fill to wholeness.

Aguinaldo said some plants only
germinate on *la luna llena.*

I must be that pearly seed, tucked
into soil for bloom by liquid light.

Constant Presence shines.
I swallow the wafer of silver-glow.

The moon in my body, by day and night,
most faithful communion.

Blaze

I don't want to make claims
like a flaunting billboard

but speak like dawn
who slips
through blues

indigo and cobalt
azure and cerulean

stars disappear
and
somewhere always
blaze

I Believe

I believe in not believing everything I think.

When thoughts are my only means to an end,
I tangle in sweaty bed sheets.

Night crows linger; "Do you believe in God?"

    "I know."

I know a woodpecker skull,
the hummingbird heartbeat,
a symphony of crickets.

I know the hushed texture of an alpine lake,
the peppered marriage of cinnamon and clove,
the generous shudder after weeping.

I know the grainy sway of a fiddle,
the ghost of your fingers on my collarbone,
the caress of just washed sheets.

I believe through these great tangibles to the unseen.

I believe all not labeled "God" is part of God.

Maybe those discarded pieces are what we long for most?

I believe we should laugh about all this much more.

I believe God is nestled in the sacred crinkle of crow's feet
around an elder's pooled eyes.

I believe joy lines are etched from canals of tears,
rivers through clay.

I believe my ancestors are written in the furrows
on my Mother's forehead.

And God is there too.

I believe that since we all touch in the secret river—

this poem,
her laugh,
that woodpecker,
those tears,
the fiddle hum—

are all prayer healing the great-grandmothers
and the unborn.

I believe that my children's faces will be a canvas of peace.

How I inhabit my body will show them what I believe.

I lie down in clover, the field beyond beliefs.

My Poems Know

what my body knows
that beyond the churned mass
of loyal neural roads,
there is a field where lupines grow.

Go often lay low and listen.
Words are on the breeze, a murmur
between pillars of grass
and each muscle's throb.

Don't turn from what rustles
unseen in a company of fescue and vetch.
Memories will rise from your shoulders
like a kaleidoscope of small russet butterflies.

Trust their flight path, follow
don't bring a net.
You will be brought where you need to be,
when there, again listen.

Dissolve into each petal
of the waiting queen anne's lace.
Your story, their story, the story
is intricately woven through each tissue.

Breathe in a hundred flowers.
Pollen will dust every cell
so your page will be covered.

An Ache for Voice

A speechless moon greets my fatigue
and asks nothing, I am to be hosted.
Silence removes layers and begins the story.

In school my sister got perfect attendance.
Once a week I was hosted by the nurse.
My sore throat or headache stretched
toward truth. I needed to ask the questions
that weren't on worksheets, with their known
right or wrong answer.
I think she knew, the nurse with kind eyes,
she saw through the layer of symptoms
scrawled on paper to my real need.
She let me sit on the cot so I could attend
to sparkling dust lit by a shaft of sun stretched
across the tile floor. In that sanctuary of permission
I learned to host all within me.

My body is a host.
Tiny-guests spiral messages in lymph.
All they know is an ache for voice. I stretch
to hear the greater invitation through fog layers.

Light is always in movement illuminating desire.
Attend to the cycles.

At nineteen, awakened to the celestial rhythms,
I asked in despair
why the monthly hosting of the great sky dance
had not been attended to all my life.

How had I not known?
As vernal women we convened at full moon
to remove layers of clothes
and old shame stretched tight.
We biked through opal night, stretching
our nakedness, bathed in one fervent curiosity.
Is the only pathology our separation
from layered connections?
Micro-organisms, dusted light, moon skin.
All hosted by the One Who Knows—
whose communion with us is through attending.

Attend is *to* and *stretch*. Words are hosted syllables,
resonators for the Center.
To arrive at the core you must know
all hallowed layers.
This layer is with me now.
I will attend.

Lake

When I remember
I am container.

Breath
  pours
    down
      each
        cascading
          rib.

Pelvic basin holds.

I am

water stilled.

When You Asked My Body

if it fears death.

The question

    fell

through me.

Old hooks have rusted away.

No where to get caught.

Puzzled ones
clutching old pain
watch as its heft

lands easy on
placid waters.

Ripples expand

    replying

all is well.

The Need for Wings

I see my ancestors as boxes
    on a narrow road.

Years of contortion into casts
    not their own—

the angular, the square,
    little room for curves.

I am emerging
    from walled lines.

I bend, arc, see and say
    there is more than this.

Show us,
    they beg.

I pick up my pen.
    I will write us wings.

How?!

the mind clomps
about in serious boots.

    Playfully,

a white feather answers

    unfurling from
      my shoulder blade.

Mend

Who bears the wound?

a little girl
in a tattered garment

How does she heal?

the Ancient One
mends with Light

Whisper from Bones

"One thing about carrying candles: you cannot go fast."
Spoken steady from my mother as light circles
her holding hand and flickers over cherry wood.
The past whispers,
mothers and daughters have midwifed this same flow,
bearers of light from darkness to darkness.
How do we relearn?
Ancient bones rattle the question

resounding through the marrow of my bones.
I want to press my lips into the lurid yellow fat,
fasting from all else,
nourished by the darkness
where blood cells are made.
In science class we drew cells.
I pictured lifesavers bobbing in the flow
of my red river veins. "Speed is about survival," whisper

my tiny companions. In fight-flight capillaries whisper
urgency through limbs. Something is wrong.
Muscles pull bones; run from buffalo herd,
cop car, arrow's pierce, bullets flow,
your open hand, my own ardent light. I hold fast
to the primal story. Ancestor's needles sew circles
into the tapestry of beliefs.
No moon tonight, sky a dark gift.

No more hiding. I run toward this darkness.
"To run in the dark you must go slow." Whispers
barn owl, grey wolf, swift fox—
the great family of things circling.

I am in the valley with Ezekiel, prophesying; dry bones
knock against all that is in me.
I want to run fast. I want to hide.
I breathe slow into the flow

of fear, wind in lungs flows a hope, unraveling darkness.
To foretell what is to come, I fast from time.
Wisdom whispers from a grandmother's candle;
"these bones will rise and form a circle."

Come from the four winds, breath encircles the promise;
all staunched will again flow.
Flesh quilts, knit ligaments, sinew sewn to bone
bodies dawn from the dark carrying light,

they whisper through the valley, chanting slow: "Hold fast
to this circle within. Birthed of darkness,
each flame flows from deep time, whispers
to bones afraid. All marrow is created of light. Hold fast!"

Blood Sisters

Before we bled, we pricked fingers
to press together small knowing.
We are alive we sang to a blushed sky
and any who would hear
our hearts under breast buds.
We were heard by crimson women
singing the hymn of fire and birth.
Blood sisters teaching us
to dance with the moon,
to tend pomegranate wombs
lined with life-jewels
and of monthly flow from lips.
Lips that part for arrival—
a rose can open and open
if there is tender light.
Blood of a body to meet breath,
bloomed cry, *I am alive.*

Thoughts On My Mind

A woodpecker wraps her tongue around her brain
to temper brash exploration into tree core, an ingenious
cavity between skull and thought,
length of tongue hugging gray matter.

Don't believe me?
Truth is, I read it on a popsicle stick after eating away
the Creamsicle's orange filled with delight.
I wish I could arch my tongue
going, going, gone into wet mystery.
How would it feel to hold the center?
Ivan taught me that the mind is more than we think,
that memories are improvised jazz.
Coltrane's saxophone trills across 86 billion brain cells
knitting together remembered fragments.
When the past visits, I want to lift out twisted tissues
and croon them lullabies making it all better.
But they tell me the brain has no pain receptors.
Not able to "wrap my mind around this," my heart opens.
I want my 50,000 thoughts per day to come
from the palace of my heart.
For I have lived years in the creases of the negative:
Quit it! Stop! Shouldn't! Failure!
Underwater it can be hard to see
that we are filled with all we need, vehicles for wonder.
I want to walk the 400 miles of my mind
stretched from Fresno to Monterey
crossing all the places I have been afraid to go.
You can come with me for they say no two minds are alike,
and two heads are better than one.

Migration

—Merced Wildlife Refuge

From the unseen an arriving shimmer,
a blizzard of snow geese, cacophony of white
land as one on shallow water.
A congregation of wings—thousands
of feathers in all states of experience—
lift, open, tuck and preen.

Never silent, they converse with a gentle wind
and a sky stretched clear as longing.
Some places are to pass through,
carrying where you have been, only
a distant knowing of where you must go.

With a great chorus of movement
the gaggle rise bellowing and we do too,
compelled by this remarkable ordinary.
I stand, winged-shadows fly through me,
waking tired desire.

How far I have been from the shape of myself,
following the flock of voices, not my own.
The body is made to know where we must go.

Space for Soul to Catch Up with Body

Trains enter towns through the backdoor.
Factories loom like rusted dinosaur fossils.
Backyards reveal half-filled swimming pools,
Christmas tree skeletons piled next to tomato seedlings,
hung laundry surrenders, fabric wind,
from a grandmother's hands.
Engines trundle into stations, children run
throwing pebbles, flying feet.
Leaning against time, that group of old men
take it all in, what do they gather?
A weathered cowboy tips his hat in Santa Fe,
his wrinkles titter and creak.
I needed to cross the land I travel.
Kansas sky and corn, Minnesota blue woods.
Lakeshore Limited, California Zephyr, Desert Wind
Hours map through framed windows,
old stories play against new backdrops.
Constant movement in chambered stillness.
Lovers sleep coiled on seat cushions,
legs loosely twined. Nearby a toddler,
nose squished to glass, her Mama knits.
We all travel together, gentle sway
carries us in our belovedness,
so that soul and body arrive as one.

2

Waxing

Dizzy Moon

Seventy-two moons have cycled since I met you.
An August moon greeted our first seeing,
when you glimpse your soul in another.
I told you of healing by moon-glow biking naked and free.
You told me the moon made you dizzy,
gazing upon grandeur feeling yourself small.
We sang "Helplessness Blues" and fell in love.
Six years of falling, the moon constant in the dark.
We have always seen the light in each other
illuminating a future vision, shadow-play,
figures and dreams cast on a tent wall.
We followed the moon, would she be brighter
over desert, mountains or meadow?
Could we join her rhythms?
Would we then be able to live light?
But the moon is the same everywhere.
I stood in a clearing in the Cascades, a golden-moon
rising low streaked by the silhouette of fir and pine,
I had to leave.
When I found the moon in my body I returned.
I thought we found the same light,
at last ready to shimmer together.
I dreamed of marrying you under a full gaze,
dancing purple and auburn, fiddle and drum.
Tonight in Ohio under soft-glow,
I am alone with fireflies and memories
ripping threads from a dress.

Tutoring

Between commas, you tell these sapling girls,
nearly women, about love.

How easy it is to ignore
the small voice within that knows,
its lift can be a single feather forsaken in a storm.

How through unbroken gales, it is always there,
tattered maybe, ragged even
but the hollow (not empty) center bends in wind.

How when you listen and follow each
slight and mighty knowing, it is marvelous,
each feather necessary for flight.

Their wide young hearts beat in their eyes,
and they tell you in English class
they are learning about symbolism,

(shyly, we bend close as if a baby bird
has nested on worksheets, to look upon
and whisper to not wake)

that means you must go deeper than what you see.

You tell them yes,

how you must.

Salt

We once drove through
the Great Salt Lake. Windows down,
heat blasted our anthem, the flats
rouge, grit and bitter blue,

seasoned with the tang of water dried.
I wanted to get out of the car
and tramp through the minerals,
my feet crunching through

each layer of story.
But warned not to turn back,
we drove fast, you turned the music up,
and the pillar grew higher, as silent pain

hardened my salted spine.
No water till the horizon,
I could not leave my offering of salt.

Puzzle

Our feet twined in hope
while we hunched over a puzzle
that snow-blind night.

Wondering could this quirky piece,
a shape so particular
brushed the cavernous blue
of trees at days dim,
fit within the sun-washed
crook of another.

We scattered our story on the wooden table
to clump like-pieces together—
inky luster of raven wing,
rust of foxtail, speckled dun of fawn—
each bright and shadowed thing.

We tried to join, kissing the rim
of this piece and that,
sure with understanding
an image would match the one
imprinted on our hearts.

Our shoulders curled in question
long past that frigid night.
Spring promised nettle and violet
before the wither to unspeakable heat.

The attempt abandoned,
some cardboard bent

from effort, most pieces
lost on the floor.

During a searing July downpour
I put the fragments away—
raven glimmer, fox flash
and deer glance.
I see the whole.
The story now fits
because it does not need to,
it cannot.

To Tell Our Story

I wet a page
my brush strokes
     skin to skin,
     two colors.
I tilt the paper's end—
     you flowed into me,
          I flowed into you,
there was bloom and mud.

All colors come from earth,
rock scraped against rock.

When paper dries, we say
     the painting is done,
but each time I hold this weighted
page to a specific light
     I see more.

Lips search the canyons
of years, rolled into one another.
     Mixed hues,
all for the right word
     to empty the measure of hurt and love
     from our twined tongues.

I must stop our long wrestle
     with words.

Necessary Abandon

I gave myself to water. I became
    a bough of snow in a High Sierra meadow, in wait
for April to begin the flute-solo of water in motion.
    One drop gliding down a single sun tarnished note,
soon joined by the crystal choir of a million others,
    taken by gravity of desire to find
each naked pleat of earth to caress.
    Gradually the crease torn open. Droplets unite as one,
a language of satin rippled with expectation.
    Then communion with granite.
No part of the other untouched.
    We love with necessary abandon
not able to embody what we do not yet know.
    That one will fall leaving the other at cascading heights.
What moments ago was solid has reached its end.
    All water can do is follow
the reckless roar straight down,
    wherever it leads, a frothed pool or ample mist.
Always somewhere, always reunited with the flow,
    most often by way of dark earth.
The river pulses wide into the Valley of need.
    When a poppy sun cries through once ice
you can see each glinted stone.

Turning 30 at Muir Rock I Remember the Other Stones

I.

Amber ribbons of snowmelt carry me
as I lay on Muir's rock quaking in gratitude with aspen.
The canyon womb has birthed me
again and again into this life.

II.

As young girls we crushed pine sap and bamboo
in carved bowls of rock.
Imagining Mayan princesses
also at home on these soft needles
also dreaming the only dream I knew—
of babies they would carry on their hips
the husbands they would love.

III.

Our flashlights carved a tunnel through the pines.
Teenagers charged with hormones and midnight.
Seth held my hand as we lay
on top of the Sierras the Milky Way in our hearts.

IV.

At twenty, each bone starved, I sought solid rock.
Found on a shelf of granite in an Andean meadow,
glaciers and *cordillera* butterflies revealed
the invitation from love to Love. I said yes.

V.

Boulder to boulder, I followed you down river
for a yes, for you to want me in the surefooted way
your lithe limbs trusted the leap over coursing water.
Your body said no, the scrape down mossy stone stings.

VI.

After the summer storm rain drips from layers.
I stacked shale in a spiral. Memory and
loss snaking through the streambed.
Flat stones heavy with desire of dreams
I didn't know to dream.

VII.

Today wedded to flow and ground I need nothing more.
I sit up in the quiet riverway of light.
Space made when frozen waters expand cracking sandstone.
With the sun at this angle each broken/whole stone
come to rest on silt and years is enough.

Stone

Facing my Goliath,
the giant looming
impossible,

I tremble inside
armor laden
with the past,
shield up
to this moment,
the future heavy
with the unknown.

I want to trust
like women before,
who reached
into the brook
to select
a few small stones.

No shield,
I carry
pieces of earth
worn smooth
by the conversation
of movement and time,
touching each stone now.

When I See You Again

"What if we joined our sorrows?
What if that is joy?"
—Ross Gay

I will speak to you of wings.
Of how I have found a hundred feathers

on the sidewalks and wooded paths
of my heart since I saw you last.

How I have lifted each one by the hollow stem
to read the particular story of release.

Last summer you lifted
a blood red cardinal feather to the muggy light,

showing me how the red strands matted with saliva
meant this bird was attacked by another.

You dropped the feather
in the dewy grass as you walked away.

Some sorrows must be gazed upon together
before any praise or gratitude

for the beauty of red wings that once flew
is spoken.

Eclipse

You always walked fast,
I was a foot-fall behind
to follow your bright light.
My radiance enveloped
in your shadow, my own dark
keeping me there.

I kept trying to match our steps,
I'd run to catch your hand.

Pitch

I am the moth
wing trapped in the shut blinds
crushed between slats of moonlight

hours of battered flying
over and over
trying to free myself

the world the distorted inch
between cold glass and sliced plastic
frantic effort until night is pitch

stuck

no sliver of star to guide
bruised and trembling
I surrender in wait with my scars

till I hear the first bird sing
the courage of another voice
reminds me of my own

intact deep within my weary wing

Sighted Dark

Jesus said, "What can I do for you?"
The blind man said, "My Teacher, I want to see."
—Mark 10:51

As a distant train groans
across midnight, I wrestle
with what I cannot yet see.

In this gnawing dark,
I am with blind Bartimaeus,
huddled on the sidelines
of the rushed world.

Fully there yet hardly seen,
he could listen
to swept street-talk, to words
between those spoken, to words
not intended to be heard.

Maybe he needed the years
of sighted-dark,
ghosted shapes alchemized
not touched by direct gaze.

Such that when he heard
The Healer's question
there was stillness within
the teeming depths.

What he needed
had been formed,

the courage to name
his pure desire
to the One
who would see it.

The Question I Need to Ask

Can you describe my smell?

When you love someone you want to taste them.

Whatever their peached aroma,

this becomes your new fragrance,

wild with the slightest whiff.

You rarely showered and I loved your smell,

musk and soil, exactly what a human should smell like.

Wild to press my face into the salty crease of your neck,

just the right height for our bodies to align.

We spoke of wild communion but sometimes

it was like I was saving you from something.

I saw it in your crazed clinging eyes.

I was a body to dispense into when needed.

Muzzling my *no* I turned over.

Unaware there were shores of pleasure we were far from.

I do not blame you or myself. I grieve it all.

Seen, unseen, known, unknown

that prevented us from giving each other

the only thing we were wild to give and receive.

The Questions I am Terrified To Ask

Did you ever really love me?

Or

were you more in love

with how I loved you?

With the idea of loving me?

The Weeping

Held by sycamore roots
and every woman,
I weep you out of my body
till tears course clear.
Rage drums my bones.
Your pain inflamed
the space between my cells
entered my everything
took and took.
Unaware I was dry
your needs chafed my orchid soul.
We swallowed and each left longing.
Once you called me angel,
moonlight loving our bare legs, and said
let's spend a whole day in bed together.
Six years of days and we never did.
Today my organs pound earth.
I bury everything pain prevented
into moldered leaf layer—
my forgiveness,
my yes,
to the life that calls me angel
where pleasure caresses each cell.

I used to say you helped me grow.
Alone I have chosen
again and again to gather
my shredded shadow
and walk her into the Light.

Seaglass

I collect seaglass
     watching sand for a glint
          of amber, cobalt or green.

I save these time polished bits
     on my window ledge
          far from the sea, still drinking sun.

We are here because something broke;
     waters, hearts, glass.
          A thin crack or shattered crash,

strewn fragments
          tumble on tides till worn.
          Sharp glass softened,

made new, we say, healed.
     But because it was cut
          there will always be an edge.

Through the Web

Come morning,
the field is drenched.

I circle the rim gleaning wild rye,
broom sedge and cordgrass.

Stems heavy with drink
bent from dew and late rain.

I raise a green blade to my lips.
The summer storm rolls through me.

I pray my thundering questions
pool like droplets on thirsty stalks.

Wet by the presence but
separate from their weight,

sprung back to shape at the release,
each gem traveled to earth. Lightened,

I listen through the spider's web
visible when dripping with diamonds.

Both

This fury and calm
alive in the same body,
the flare
the steady,

    touch.

The lilac bush
crackled leaves clung on
while on the same bough
the generous new,

    sun fills each.

Maybe *how? why?* or *always?*
    are not the questions.

    Sorrow filled with sun.

Braiding

"We can see forever when the vision is clear."
—Cyprian Consiglio

In a house of linen and willow
I have been braiding the rose-blonde hair
of our imagined children.

While they slept on goose feathers
you and I roamed our land, dancing with
the star-fire that all our pain had grown.

Today I wake from years of dream
come to this moment
where I lie alone on cotton

in a house of my own
fully accompanied by morning sun-fire.
You are far away and at last I am right here—

vision through light of the current
and only forever. From this clarity
I brush out the tangles,

and allow hands beyond my own
to sort out silken threads
too fine for human grasping.

Our braided hopes
slip through my hands
falling into place.

Two Dragonflies

I have written many poems to release you—
of an egret alone before elegant flight,

of oak leaves in winter's pasture, of an acorn's sprout,
of mangrove roots and birds, so many birds—

today asks for another way to let go.
I watch two dragonflies, flit of dazzled blue.

They weave a complex choreography,
as if connected by an invisible cord,

hovering together over murky waters, then part
cutting ties to ask the question in a new way.

With you and without you I have expanded
beyond all imagined limits. I am not afraid.

I see myself as a girl, sun soaked in creek water
moving sticks and mud from a catch between stones,

to create space for flow.

3

Full

The Orca's Grief

for the Pacific Northwest Orca Pod

For 16-moons she grew hope,
pulsed presence in her womb,
birthed in the depths
brought to light for first air.

They swam side-by-side
those six joyful minutes
mother and calf, alive
in hope's astonished waters.

Quick as dire lungs fill,
breath and hope can vanish.

Now the Great Mama holds
her beloved, laid to rest
on the slick bow of her body
lifted above the grave.

Her pod travels with her.
Weeks through cold sea,
keening blue-gray-green,
they carry the young one
when she cannot bear the weight.

Miles to acceptance, ever alone,
always accompanied,
in movement with grief
through each wave's crest.
When there she will arrive,
release into luminous deep.

Instructions

After Jean Janzen

For August
As heat closes with silence, you must
swell like lemons globed green.

In time
you will eat sunlight.

For September

Weep with willows who reach
arms into gaunt canals,

let discomfort cradle you,
life grows in this desert.

For October

Wildfires will burn bones to char.
Your mother sees your ashen face—

you can no longer masquerade
to please every masked man.

For November

Join hushed let-go with gingko and oak,
flamed carpets remind

you have all you need
in spiced decay.

For December

Say yes to treasured pondering
with Mary in the heart cave.

The unknown is oxygen for soil's womb,
expect birth.

I Wondered About Sunday

aware of the long loneliness.
With hours for sun to marinate memories
I take myself to the canal. Here
last year's snow speaks the fluency of spring.

I clutch for the hand that is not here.
Skin to assure me that I exist, will keep existing.
My heart is paper-thin eucalyptus bark
exposed layers in various stages of come-in/let-go.

Beautiful because it is raw.
Curled strips of bruised pink,
lavender and muted green
float like neglected ribbons
into this moment, the next, and another.

I peel back a strip of bark, slightly damp,
perfume of baked dust, mint and honey.
I hold this new canvas with open hands,
cradled in my existence.

Magnolia and Pine

From one window
I see a magnolia
from the other a pine.

I believed health
was a bloom.

Now, I learn
golden sap rises
like tears from a root.

Tear Medicine

Tears are tincture, the whole foraged
for swampy infusion steeped within
till ripened to medicine.

I drink this salty healing.
My tongue honors
each crystal of story as it flows.

I catch wept waters
in cobalt glass
labeled with flourished script:

Soul-Weep
Rattling of Belief Systems
on a Rainy Tuesday in Ohio

Bottled for the days when thirsty
for ground I squeeze a dropper-full
of prayers into raspberry tea.

Leaf and lime mingle the memory;
this journey will brew the medicine I need.
This damp day sacred pain is held

by Grammy-Great's handkerchief—
yellowed with dainty purple pansies
sheer from years of intimate touch.

Eden's Drought

I forgot the ballad of water joining land,
our sorrow the only strum.
Drought is slow death, shroud of smoky sin
keening between the mountains.
"In the red," the newspapers say:
"Air unfit to breathe."
Bodies are made for taking in.
Valley lungs are dust.
Kin of *Adamah*, we are created
of dust and water, Spirit breathed life.
Alive in this arid garden, my mother prays,
saving dishwater to anoint
persimmon, grapevine, and fig leaf.
At autumn's first rain, January late,
relief falls by night, a moon sings off every surface.
Tomorrow our grief will breathe clear sky.

Holy Water

By night the trees are blessed,
christened with life's elixir.
A row of droplets, tiny pearls, dangle
on a baby girl's earlobe, baptism at first light.
I take a gleaming bead from bare apricot limb,
to wet my forehead, lips, heart, root.

A priest blesses the bowed masses,
water flung from a cut sapling.
In Peru crowds line up
at the side-door of the cathedral,
with empty *Inca Kola* bottles to be filled.
The devoted, the thirsty.

A simple spigot pours from the stone temple
labeled with painted signs,
Agua Santa.
One-by-one we fill our need,
reaching heavenward with
each splash down.

Moths Drink the Tears of Sleeping Birds

Moths drink the tears of sleeping birds.
Sterling wings dipped in moonlight

quake like aspen over the winged other,
hovering in wait for the night-pearl.

Does the sleeper know
of the visitation, the taking, the touch?

The precise open and shut of a wing
ripples through chaos.

The same for this tear?
Shed, given, tasted, received.

Reunion

Heart cells keep alive absent of their host
will continue to beat.

Almost as if the tree has held vigil
till this December day
for my knotted body to press into rings,
the part of myself alive in its layers, come home.

Are the cells of my heart strewn?
Flaked off with each love and loss.

A scattered hosting in Sierra pine,
rosy Honduran coral,
Midwestern goldenrod,
and pebbles of Rhode Island shore,

and with you first firefly love,
with you caramel sun,
and you oak in Ohio.

Jewels

When you wake and the sadness is close,
and they are farther than far away.
Wander into the wide world,
where on this street light falls
on the mother pushing a stroller,
on teenagers who saunter with that droop,
and on your neighbor Jorge
as he jogs in place telling you about the marathon.
And you are taken to the creek,
where you visited the water-striders daily,
a flotilla clustered under
the wooden bridge, also coated in light.
A jeweled moon where each leg met water,
suspended on the impossible.
Afloat on delicate tension—
what we push against and what
pushes against us.
Aware this loss may always press,
you let tears come, jewels
upon which you can float
as you nod "good morning"
saying *I see you*, to each passing one.

The Way In Is Through

When not listening to the one who knows
the body can be a stone,
or soft as warm sugared-wax,
left after honey is spun from the comb.
Where does the voice live?
Somewhere deep we say, hands pressed to the solar-plexus,
the place where we lose our breathing.
When staggered backward we must let ourselves fall
into the soft/hard, from where the buzzing known beckons.
Follow the stir into the deep, dark with flighted shadows.
Keep on toward the one you are learning is your own.
It will not be louder than the rest, but clear.
When you find the source it may be hidden by layers,
wrapped as if with fragile paper.
With care acknowledge each fold, in time
the container will loosen, unravel.
When you reach with bare hands into the center hive,
the swarm may sting.
Let the burn confirm you have lived.
Beveled cells dripped with gold-light
will reveal all you have gathered.
Years searching each blossom's depth,
you have never been alone.
Savor this honeyed-reunion with each past knowing.

All that you longed for has been so close,
speaking through each moment,
your only way in.

Conversations

All night the waves spoke.
Inhale and exhale
between earth and expanse.

We slept on a hill above to hear.
Our bodies sunk in sand, warm,
cocooned in silt.

As gloam covers twilight
my Mother and I put forth the question—
a lone owl yearning into vast blue.

Our voices the sand-speck of a star-blaze,
another turn of the conversation
since we tumbled from water.

Graced with breath after each swell,
then the pull back for silence.
Words risen from the depths to crash

against a millennia of rocks softened.
Fanned wide, the spoken glistens,
a curved line on darkened sand.

Words carried on tides of sleep
and waves of owl call.
Nothing and everything answered.

Preening

"Being alive takes time"
—Mark Nepo

Perched on a blonde ravel of driftwood
a colony of seagulls preen.

With care throughout the day
they notice what is with them.

They clean and oil,
realign each flight-feather.

Before the next wind wave
they tend to what will carry them,

releasing what is no longer needed,
a battered feather billows across the shore.

Time

In her parents' garage shafts of midday
illuminate neglect. Desert heat buckles
the aluminum roof, so dry she does not sweat.
She finds the cardboard boxes labeled, *Julia's Journals,*
and carries years of ink out to the fig-tree's shade.
Scanning penned words, her heart wanders the past.
Their names are everywhere, written on her body,
red marks on a cave wall. Then
hands pressed this page, now
simply a formation of symbols and letters.
She flattens the spine, names folded
between other names, fading in the sun.

Shadows

With sun at high-noon
our shadows seep into us,
a sliver of residual night
this inescapable companion
once beside, now walks within.
Be still, let lessons revealed
by moon-shadow
meet the bold witness.
This doesn't last long,
always surrender, the obscured
ceded to clarity, before
feathered light drapes trees
with evening's garment
woven of borrowed darkness,
laid over us in kind necessity.

Foothills

I.

The shadow on the hills,
a presence.

As if I could lift a corner of meadow
and a vast scarf, sewn of each sorrow, would rise.

I won't, I have learned
the importance of ground.

Purple velvet drapes a shoulder,
the other laid bare, streaked with sun.

The next ridge muted wine, again
followed by gold, where they meet

the fold deepens almost to nothing.
Each crease made visible because of this—

fire begging to touch soil, soil
that wants only to feel the luminous caress.

II.

All my life I have felt an almost silent,
almost constant lack, for what unfurled

did not follow the path I thought I would travel.
This exhaustion (from the miles,

each crest and fall to find the path)
has made it hard to see,

that along the undulating way,
I found union.

The spark that kisses the seed
is what brings the hillside to petaled ecstacy.

III.

No need for a path in these hills,
among cow-trails and poppies, I know

where I am, which is enough.
Held by gravity of all grown in tension

with what may flourish as shadow
and light constantly join.

4

Waning

Dust Motes Dancing in the Sunbeams

—After painting by Vilhelm Hammershøi

When painting the swath of light
did he see the room as empty or full?

Day slices through the tall window,
each frame of glass a passageway. Suspended,

I waltz with a mote on the beam.
We float through the quiet room,

in and out of sight. Speck of my discarded cells
and yours, the cat's, particles of twine and bone, sand

of stone and linen fluff, mouse mite, and brush fiber,
grain of paper and spill of ink.

In this vast room we breathe what makes us;
burnt meteorite grit, wheat chaff, gingko leaf rot,

our bones quake and let go.
Sloughed off skin spins from our bodies,

we kiss and shudder. Spilled squares slant
across the blue-gray floor. Dust settles.

Rest

To stop you must really stop.

Camphor air and nectar light,
nothing aches to be done.
Sweet rest teaches all I have desired.

Allow yourself to be held on a bed of light.
To observe the way sun
and his other flit on the washed wall.

Gaze until you cannot tell leaf from branch
space from shadow from vivid white.

See the Source
from which all dances,
then keep looking.

In the Secret World

the mourning doves also coo, the black cat stalks,
and your father nods good morning
as you emerge bleary from dream.

The left side of the bed is still cold,
and similar worries condense, clutching the cords
around your shoulders where the great cloak
of memory is draped, dense purple and velvet.

And there is a cavity of quiet astonishment,

where each rupture and rapture
is acknowledged without concern,
part of the warp and weave

each thread seen
for its tremendous significance
but not as what will save.

I join the daily ballad. I pounce with the cat,
an ebony river rippled with attention,
I ride the neurons delivering the nod of love.

I bless the loves that now dream in other beds
and roll into the middle of my own. Here
I invite each worry to lay while I embroider
peonies and star-showers into velvet.

Matter

A party of wrens splatter
their making all over the driveway,
dramatic explosions tie-dye
cement the color of ripe plums.
Unaware of this offering,
I watch them from my desk
writing my desire to be a bird.

On paper they stay afloat
in the space before
light touches matter. I wanted
home to be winged-light,
for the formless to be enough,
freed from this dramatic need
to touch and make.

Yet, I see light because it touches,
almost as it if *loves*, the bend
of branch made slick with dawn,
the umber in a feather now a flame,
and these streaks of purple
just moments ago warmed
by blood, now shining.

Why

We begin as a bundle of cells,
once the size of a poppy seed.
Created from a coming together.
Seed and ova burgeoning
with desire for form to love.

In union the two became one.
To thrive we must split,
the grand pattern revealed at our start,
divide to expand again and again.

My mother pauses between washing plates,
green scrubbie raised to dripping light,
iridescent with soap one bubble froths into
a cluster of transparent pearls.

I know why we are here she says,
"praising."
Our cells, glassy orbs, separate and bloom
in desire to be form that loves.

My sister placed a trembled hand
on her womb
when the dividing stopped
and the come-away began.

The miraculous carried by the waters,
a poppy seed on a leaf
floats across Lake Washington,
touched by evening, while cells divide.

Communion

I fill each cup. Chocolate topped with cream,
SwissMiss and Cool-Whip, the elements.

They come to the table—red-nosed toddlers,
permed grandmothers, and lanky tweens.

Light stains cloud breath, yellow-green-red,
wink in rhythm with "Santa Baby."

My vestment of bedazzled antlers
dips low as I place warmth in each cupped hand.

For less than a breath the skin of our lives
brushes against our separation, only cells between us.

We are so close to the Body.
We are so close to the Blood.

Clay

She kneels

the posture to harvest red earth
from carved riverway.
Ruby milk streams between fingers.
A round of supple clay left in her palm.
Enough to form a little bird,
simple body, beak and wing.

She kneels

placing the bird on a stone
to dry by equator sun.
Heat that grew her adobe home.
Heat that builds tawny kernels,
maize stitched into soil's open seam,
made ready in her oven of baked earth.

She kneels

her body sinks into the clay she is.

Tortilla Yellow

A departing moon floods her adobe kitchen
with egg yolk light. Fertile, this silence before,
when she can imagine the path she will take
to the cathedral with flame for two candles.
Fire and dawn stain glass, her face, the Mother's, aglow.
She kneels on packed earth
tending the same fire, prayers leap from straw.
Against the wall a sack of kernels bedded in silk.
A threadbare apron, sunflowers
mellowed to daisy, hugs her hips. She rocks
maize into masa, dough into life.
Her crucifix hangs
in the caramel cave between breasts,
swings in rhythm with nourishment.
She leans over the source to splatter lard on hot tin.
Her amber hands encircle the sacrament,
pan de la vida, each round imprinted with enough.
A row of small corn suns rise on the comal.
Her children wake hungering Mama,
small hands reach for all they need.
In the distance church bells cry *amarillo.*

Hands

Here with this knife
I slice rays of sun

time turned to sugar.
A circle of carrot rolls across wood.

Once another hand was with this knife,
liquid fire hammered to steel.

The carrot, once seed,
chosen for loam by a hand.

The board a seed, carried
by squirrel from cone to forest duff.

The cedar felled by gloved hands,
a maul cleaving growth years.

The knotted bough planed and finished
on the workbench of a man in Indiana.

I gather these rounds of root
and cook them in butter,

creamed fat, clover chewed
in an Irish meadow.

Hands once held a warm udder
milk splattered into a bucket.

Soles

Why do we map the future

by the lines on our hands

when feet are just as creased?

I trace the canyons and gullies

of my arched soles.

Not to fortune what is to come.

I see all I need of the path.

Hands listen to what is here,

fingers tip-toe magnolia skin

storied veins lit by sun.

To Hold

She cradles her longing in the great lap of now,
a landing ample and boundaried, to hold what fits.

Legs draped with pale linen her open palms stilled.
One hand to cup morning, honeysuckle light

brimming with all she needs. The other to hold night,
where in dreams she and the beloved waltz the Milky Way.

All the rest spills between fingers and over warm thighs,
drifts like flour to settle in graced crevices

of was and will be.

Advent

I dreamt of a mango tree
laden in a field of snow.

Flushed golden ornaments
tucked among waxy leaves,

flourishing in barren ice,
pregnant with joy.

I eat fruit born of the illogical.
It tastes of trust.

April Snow

April snow in Ohio
    comes down slow.
        I try to follow

one flake
    from full cloud
        to powdered ground.

In California, I taught children
    to make snow, the carpet dusted
        with white paper.

We cut into the known
    to make by taking away,
        trust of pattern in the unseen.

When flakes unfold,
    faces beam through lace.
        I relinquish effort to trace

the sky to earth path
    of a single crystal.
        What is melts on my tongue.

Summer Moon

concealed by a castle of rumpled clouds,
sheet of cotton white,
shadows dye each fold indigo.

Sky bed warm with night-knowings,
words traced on paper skin
only faded contours legible by light.

Wind blanket shifts, disrobes
bone curve of an ivory hip,
a breast of marbled light.

She is always whole.

Gentle this reveal,
to see for now
all that needs knowing.

Hunger

*"To stay on the surface of anything is to invariably
miss its message."*
—Richard Rohr

Today I am the red-throated hummingbird—
blur of beauty hovering. To survive I enter
the petaled cavern. Swaddled
in sugar-light, I go deeper. Flick
of tongue blooms at the source.
I immerse in the nectar pool
nourished by the hidden.

The Kiss

Hung over my bed, Klimt's lovers
press together in gold leaf.
Sunk in petaled splendor
he cups her astor cheek,
unseen lips, *The Kiss.*
Her toes curl on pleasure's brink.
She drapes him with her ease.
Their shut eyes are full of sight,
gold flecks overlay desire in darkness,
The Beloved caresses my face.

When You Meet Someone

who might be your love

pause while you slice the strawberries
that will soon touch their lips

and look out at the lemon tree
burnished with silent light

so that when they are here
at this kitchen table
hands sticky with berry seed

you will be able to listen
to the silence

within and under words

to hear

if you both speak
of the Light infusing
everything everything

Sweet Things

Too many hurried movements
when there are sunflowers
and peaches lazing to ripeness,
next to a jar filled with
one thousand bees drinking.
Honey I bought from Bob,
who drives a big yellow truck
with a bumper sticker—"bee happy."
This poem might never be
more than this moment.
Within the quick of questions,
the sweet things
dripping from the honeycomb
of the Real, save me
every time.

Anything Green Helps

Frayed shoes on cold pavement.
He stands at the Hwy 41 entrance ramp.
Bold sharpie on a Cheerios box—

"Anything Green Helps."

I imagine handing him a crisp granny smith apple,
a sprig of kinked parsley, a cut avocado
fruit of creamed fat.

Not in jest but in answer to his truth,
naming our profound need.

I would invite him to my backyard,
to take off our shoes on the tussle of violets
and onion grass under the Chinese elm,

to look up and see the one branch
leafed in new green.

Fall 2018

Smoke poured across the Pacific, while
on a dune above we watched a monarch die.
Mosaic of orange and black, colors to warn,

one ripped wing quavered before stillness.
"How can God stand it?" My Mother said.
We too had stopped, sunk to ground,

this shredded life heaving us to the magnitude of loss.
The Oxford Dictionary choose "toxic" as word of the year,
a year painted in flames and black lines.

Toxic, *"deeply but invisibly harmful,"*
an ancient word, the arrowhead dipped in venom,
word released, an arrow flies beyond the literal.

God is in the wing, in the ash, in the fire.
We hear ourselves say.
God is in the tear, in the word, in the shuddering last.

We raise the fragile body out of the path
for burial on the limb of a eucalyptus, to be seen,
the exquisite, the torn.

Beyond this Quaking

Before the tornado the sky, an acute bruise,
still for a long purple breath.
We go underground, entrusting the roots
circling these packed walls to hold us
should everything above leave in a tunnel of loss.

As a child, I built what I saw as solid,
triangle roofs with strong block bases,
with a shake to the sure
the wooden world clattered down.

We can see movement toward us,
when waters plague from the heavens
and the sea spins on land. Go in, go down,
curl your body around the constructed.

I was twelve when everything quaked,
a tremble for not even a breath,
the hypnotic lurch of the lamp cord, evidence
these movements were not my own making.

I want to live unafraid of what rumbles and rushes,
covered in mud and water yet rooted beyond,
so my blood will not flail when sirens call.
I want to go down walking light,
each step toward a deeper solidity, never shaken.

When

For the victims and survivors of California wildfires

When asked to survive, we rise above.
Burn or freeze.
Submerged in a pool for six hours and sixty years
they held each other, speaking saturated love.

Hearts aflame with everything and nothing to speak of.
The helicopter can take only four of yours
when asked to survive, they rose above.

To go above is not a pushing down, to let go
of your hija's hands, courage flowed tears
while they held each other, speaking
"if I don't see you again" love.

Courage begins *Cor*—our beating heart.
The rest of the word rages with passion's fire.
The shape we were made appears.
When asked to survive, we rise above.

Survive ends with live. Living starts in love
and has no end. The question a flame in your ears;
"can we hold each other, speaking our love?"

Everything now ash, free of what bound us, we see beyond.
Smoke clears.
We were asked to survive and have risen above.
Since this is not the end, we will hold each other,
speaking our love.

The Unreported News

There are no exact statistics for the number
of poppies on hillsides this year.
Prostrate in filmy petals we estimate millions,
praising bees who continue to sashay
from rosemary, to almond tree, to hive.
Snow fell in February, peach blossoms
frosted the ground in gratitude.
Here we drink melted Sierra peaks
and eat oranges luscious with July sun.
This sun with no agenda made raisin pucker,
apricot glow, avocado and fig surge.
Late light slants as my neighbors,
five brothers on a trampoline, reach joy.
We smile at each other daily
and seek wholeness in the ways we know.
In this Valley where heat can ruin
relief has always come—the last sigh of pink
breathed through palm fronds.

Translator

In woods slick with slow-light
the one who birthed me named me *Moon*.

She knows this is my hour.
In rest I become the fullness.

All day I absorb the sun
to write the reflection.

When back-lit by the sun's departure
bundled needles on the fir bough

are fresh ink marks on the page of dusk,
each line revealed.

I translate what the trees say.

Rhizome

Sugar tunnels through soil. Spun threads
weave sunlight into a tapestry of roots. Above
a stand of aspen, yellow with late-August, breathe.
Four separate columns drink nitrogen and cloud
through the straw-maze of one single rhizome.

In yoga class I press the sole of my foot
against the inside of my calf,
balanced with arms overhead.
The teacher tells us to imagine
our planted foot as a root growing down
through carpet and wood, cement and stone
to join the riverway of nourishment.

I am here at the desk of the woods
to find the taproot. My shovel, a pen,
I dig through layers of page
for the word that is my own,
that touches everything.

Pentecost

Bushes burn with red-bud at twilight.
Wind-breath speaks
the forest crowned with flamed leaves.
Every language recognized here.

Fire is tongue of the soul.
The soul is heat of the body.

Bodies are always burning,
luminous unspeakable beauty,
each of us a glint in this radiant whole.

Gifted with breath, we join the wind.
Spirit rush from lungs
kindles everything spoken.

Humpback Harmonies

After a cello performance by Eugene Friesen

The cello and whale ride waves in a haunted duet.
On a held note the sleek body breeches,
in one massive eye everything stops.

We breathe, you return
and fill the ocean cathedral with aching tones.
Eugene's body wraps the cello, stroking

the chamber of golden echoes.
Space and string all that is needed,
eyes closed he breathes, and everything moves.

We don't know why the whale gives song.
No need to know. We sing for wonder, for joy,
of the instrument we all are.

Vessels

I watch the choreography of pigeons
across the stage of shapeless dawn.

How can one describe the symphony
of wings but as rejoicing.

I hear the same notes sung
by three blue jars on my window ledge,
aglow with lids off filled with afterlight.

Could it be everything is a vessel of praise?

A spark rises from chalky coals,
our prayers are breath on embers
heat from lungs inviting
flame to recognize flame.

All fire sings the same song.

Silvered green/purple iridescence,
head feathers alit; these common birds,
that blue glass, our ignited souls—

we are all swirling caldrons of light.

Acknowledgments and Credits

These words could not have emerged if it weren't for the lives that have woven into my own. For each life known and named and unknown, unnamed I am grateful.

Z, our weaving is a complex tapestry, the Light within my threaded self honors the Light within you.

This book is born of healing. Thank you to Perla, Naomi Solane, and Doug Frank for your presence with all my parts. To my parents for being a haven. To Kat, Emie, Rachel, and Christie for your sister-friendship. To my extended family for your prayers and support. And to Ivan, for seeing me when I needed to be seen.

Thank you to Jean Janzen for naming me as a poet and for modeling the poetic-life of beauty and belovedness.

Thank you to Lee Herrick, your poetry class at Fresno City College is where I said *yes* to the fire.

Thank you to St. Matthew's Episcopal Church and the Saturday Morning Poetry group for entrusting me with space to play. Joe and Marie thank you for being family.

Working with Cascadia/DreamSeekers has been a delight and thing of ease. Thank you to Michael A. King for bringing the book to form with such care and to Jeff Gundy for your thoughtful encouragement which has made this a better book.

Thank you to Katerina Friesen, Suella Gerber, Kevin Aldridge, Lynn Baker, Rhonda Langley, Jon Stolsfuz, Thomas Baker-Swann, and Jean Janzen for spending time with earlier versions of the manuscript.

Thomas, with you I am home.

Credits

Thank you to CommonWord for publishing "Happiness," "Stone," and "Pentecost"; the *Journal of Mennonite Writing* for previous versions of "Sighted-Dark," "Faithful Moon," and "Velvet Communion"; WatershedDiscipleship.net for previous versions of "Holy Water," "When," and "Eden's Drought."

The Author

Julia Baker Swann was born in Rhode Island and has many places she calls home. Much of her childhood was spent in Honduras and her teenage years in Fresno, California. The both/and of joy and poverty in Honduras and the harsh and subtle beauty of the Central Valley deeply infuse her work.

She completed undergraduate studies in Writing, Women's Studies and Art at Goshen College and has post-graduate studies in Somatic Internal Family Systems Therapy with the Center for Self Leadership. She has run her own art and poetry business *Gleanings* since 2012, sending subscribers original art and poems in the mail. Julia was poet-in-residence at St. Matthew's Episocal Church in Westerville, Ohio, for the spring and summer of 2018. She is poetry editor of *Geez Magazine*.

She has had poems published in *Common Word*, *The Journal for Mennonite Writing*, *Watershed Discipleship.net*, and *The Crucible* and has self-published two chapbooks, *Gleaning the Edges* and *Blue Praise*. This is her first poetry collection.

Julia lives with her husband Thomas in the Whitewater River watershed in Richmond, Indiana, where she is completing an MA in Theopoetics and Writing at Bethany Theological Seminary.